The Adventures of Robin Hood

*Retold from the Howard Pyle original
by John Burrows*

Illustrated by Lucy Corvino

Sterling Publishing Co., Inc.
New York

Library of Congress Cataloging-in-Publication Data Available

2 4 6 8 10 9 7 5 3 1

Published by Sterling Publishing Co., Inc.
387 Park Avenue South, New York, NY 10016
Copyright © 2005 by John Burrows
Illustrations copyright © 2005 by Lucy Corvino
Distributed in Canada by Sterling Publishing
$^c/_o$ Canadian Manda Group, 165 Dufferin Street
Toronto, Ontario, Canada M6K 3H6
Distributed in Great Britain and Europe by Chris Lloyd at Orca Book
Services, Stanley House, Fleets Lane, Poole BH15 3AJ, England
Distributed in Australia by Capricorn Link (Australia) Pty. Ltd.
P.O. Box 704, Windsor, NSW 2756, Australia

Printed in China
All Rights Reserved
Design by Renato Stanisic

Sterling ISBN 1-4027-2266-4

CONTENTS

Robin Hood Becomes an Outlaw

Many years ago in England, when good King Henry II sat on the throne, a famous outlaw lived in Sherwood Forest near the town of Nottingham. His name was Robin Hood.

No man ever lived who could shoot an arrow like the strong young six-footer with the blazing blue eyes. No friends ever lived like the merry fellows who roamed the forest with Robin, playing games of archery and hunting deer. The country people loved to tell the story of how Robin became an outlaw. It happened like this.

When Robin was just eighteen, the Sheriff of Nottingham offered a prize for the best archer in the land. Robin felt sure he could win, so he picked up his best bow and his best arrows and set off through Sherwood Forest.

It was springtime, and the flowers bloomed. The birds sang in the trees, which gladdened Robin's heart. He whistled and hummed as he hurried through the woods.

Presently, Robin came upon a group of men beneath an old oak tree. A big man wearing an eye patch hailed him. "Hello, little lad! Where are you going with your toy bow and baby arrows?"

That made Robin angry. "My bow and arrows are as good as yours," he said. "I am going to Nottingham town, where I will compete with other good men for a fine prize."

Another man said, "Oh! Listen to the lad! Boy, you're too young to grow a beard, but you brag about competing with good stout men! You're too weak to pull a bowstring!"

Robin grew *very* angry. "Look yonder at that herd of deer. I'll bet you three hundred pounds that I can shoot the strongest buck dead."

The man with the eye patch chuckled. "I'll bet you three hundred pounds that you don't hit *anything*."

Robin strung his bow and placed the notch of an arrow over the string. Drawing the feather end back to his ear, he aimed and shot. The arrow flew through the air toward the strongest deer in the herd. It leapt but could not dodge the arrow. The deer fell dead to the ground.

"Ha!" Robin cried. "How do you like that shot, good fellow? I know what my bet was, and I want my three hundred pounds."

Furious, the eye-patch man roared, "I'll pay you nothing. Get out of here before I beat you until you can't walk!"

Another man shouted, "You killed one of the king's deer! His men will cut your ears off!"

"Grab him!" cried a third man.

"No," argued a fourth man. "Let him go. He's just a boy."

Robin said nothing. He turned away and began walking.

All would have been well, but the man with the eye patch notched an arrow and aimed at Robin. "I will hurry the boy along," he muttered. Then he loosed his arrow.

The arrow missed Robin's head by inches. In self-defense, Robin quickly turned and shot back.

"You said I was no archer! Now say so again!" Robin shouted. The arrow flew straight to the man's heart. He fell forward on the ground.

Robin ran through the woods as fast as he could. The happiness he had felt earlier was gone. "Oh," he thought, "I wish he had never said one word to me. I wish I had never walked down that path. I will carry this pain with me for the rest of my life!"

That was how Robin came to live in the forest as an outlaw. A man had died by his hand, and he had poached one of the king's deer. The Sheriff of Nottingham himself vowed to catch Robin.

Over time, Robin met other men who had fled to the forest. Some had shot deer because their families were starving. Others had been cheated of their land and money. All had been unjustly declared outlaws. Within a year, they had chosen Robin as their leader. They vowed to fight evil men and promised never to harm a child or a woman.

The people of Nottingham soon learned to trust Robin and his men, praising him and telling tales of his adventures in Sherwood Forest. Those tales are told to this day.

CHAPTER 1

Robin Hood Meets His Right-Hand Man

One morning, Robin Hood awoke restless. He ran down to the brook, where his men were washing. "We have had no adventures for two whole weeks," he said. "I am going into the forest to see what fun I can find. If I need you, I will blow my bugle three times. When you hear that sound, run to it as fast as you can."

As Robin set out on his adventure, the birds sang in the trees. He passed storekeepers on their way to Nottingham town. Meeting a pair of pretty girls, he stopped to chat with them. He continued on his way and saw a knight in shining armor.

The path ended at the edge of a river. A narrow footbridge, just wide enough for a single man, crossed the stream. As Robin stepped onto the bridge, he saw a tall stranger on the other side. "Step aside and let me pass," called Robin Hood.

"No," boomed the stranger. "Step aside and let *me* pass, for I am the better man."

"We shall see about that," Robin shouted. "Keep standing where you are, and you'll soon find an arrow sticking through your ribs."

The stranger shouted back, "I will tan your hide if you so much as touch the string of that bow!"

"You bray like a donkey," laughed Robin, "but I can shoot an arrow clean through you faster than you could raise your staff."

"*You* bray like a coward," the stranger

retorted. "You stand there with a good bow, while I have nothing but a wooden staff."

"I have never been called a coward before," Robin said. "I'll cut myself a staff, and we'll see who the better man is."

"Oh, ho," the stranger replied, "I will happily wait for you." He leaned on his staff, whistling, as Robin walked into the forest.

Robin cut a strong oak staff, straight and flawless. As he stripped away the stems and leaves, Robin studied his opponent, who stood a full head taller, at least seven feet. Robin's shoulders were broad, but the stranger's were at least two palm breadths broader.

Still, Robin was sure he would win. "I have my staff, strong and tough," he shouted. "If you dare, meet me in the middle of the bridge. The first one to fall in the brook loses."

The stranger twirled his staff above his head

so quickly that it whistled in the air. "I can't wait!"

Robin stepped quickly onto the bridge and charged at his opponent. He faked a strike at the stranger's body, then aimed a blow at his head. It surely would have tumbled the tall stranger into the water, but he blocked it. The stranger struck back, and Robin blocked that blow. At the end of an hour, each man was bruised and sore.

Finally, Robin struck the stranger hard in the ribs. The stranger teetered for a second. Then he caught his balance and swung his staff hard at Robin's head. The blow made Robin's ears ring. He grew angry and attacked the stranger. But the stranger blocked and hit Robin again. Robin splashed into the water.

As Robin spluttered, the stranger laughed.

Robin began laughing, too. "There's not a man in all of England who can fight like that."

The stranger said, "There's not a man in all of

England who can take a beating like you did."

Robin shook the water from his horn and blew three times. In a few moments, he and the stranger heard the sound of men crashing through the woods. Will Stutely arrived first. "Good master—you're wet from head to toe!"

"That big fellow there," Robin said. "He gave me a beating and dunked me in the water."

"Then he'll get beaten and dunked himself," said Will. "Get him, boys!" Twenty men leapt at the tall stranger.

"No, no, stop! He is a good, honest man!" Robin shouted. "Good fellow, will you join my band of men? Each year, you will earn forty pounds plus three suits of Lincoln green."

The stranger scratched his head. "I will join you only if you can shoot an arrow better than you can fight with a staff."

Robin told Will to cut a strip of white bark four inches wide and set it on a distant oak tree. "Hit that mark if you call yourself an archer."

The stranger took up a bow. "If I miss, you can beat me black and blue with a bowstring."

The stranger shot. His arrow flew so straight that it struck the target in the center. "There," said the stranger. "See if you can do better than that."

Robin raised his bow. "We shall see if I do better," he said. He let the arrow fly. It zipped straight through the air and split the stranger's arrow to splinters.

"I have never seen a shot like that in my whole life!" the stranger exclaimed in wonder.

"Then my band has a new member today," said Robin. "What is your name?"

The stranger said, "Men call me John Little."

Will looked up at the giant man. "John Little?" he laughed. "I think we shall call you Little John." Robin kept Little John at his right hand because he had never met a stronger, braver man.

CHAPTER 2

The Shooting Match in Nottingham Town

The Sheriff of Nottingham had tried to catch Robin Hood, but Robin roamed freely through Sherwood Forest, and the people laughed at the sheriff. He vowed to hang Robin Hood from the highest tree in Nottingham.

The sheriff knew that no man would go after Robin alone. He himself feared Sherwood Forest. Then it came to him in a flash. He would set a trap. The sheriff would host a shooting match in Nottingham town and offer a fine prize. "When Robin Hood and his rogues come to the match, he will be in my grasp," the sheriff thought.

Robin soon heard the news. "Ho, fellows. The Sheriff of Nottingham has announced a shooting match in Nottingham town. The best archer will win a bright golden arrow. I want to win. The prize is so rich, and our sweet sheriff himself will present it. Get ready, lads!"

Young David of Duncaster jumped to his feet. "Robin, I have just come from the Blue Boar Inn. People say the match is a trap."

Robin did not fear the sheriff. "We will meet sneakiness with sneakiness," he said. He told his men to wear disguises. Some would dress in the robes of a friar. Others would don the tattered clothes of a beggar. Each man would hide a sword beneath his costume. "How do you like my plan, merry men?" Robin cried out.

Everyone in Nottinghamshire attended the contest. The archers gathered in a tent near the range. The sheriff and his wife took their seats above it. Then the silver bugles announced the beginning of the match.

The sheriff leaned forward, searching for Robin Hood. He had never seen Robin, but he knew that Robin and his men wore Lincoln green. No one was dressed in Lincoln green. "He may still be here. He will be among the ten in round two, or I don't know him at all," the sheriff thought.

The archers shot the first round. Never before had anyone in Nottingham seen such shooting. Only three arrows missed the center ring of the target. At the last shot, the crowd shouted, "Hurrah!"

The ten men who had shot best remained on the range. Six were famous throughout the land. Two others were from merry Yorkshire. A stranger in blue said he came from London town. The last man was dressed all in red. He wore a patch over his right eye.

The second round began. As each man took

aim, the crowd fell silent. When the last man shot, everyone again shouted and clapped.

Now three men remained. One was Gilbert o' the Red Cap, another was the stranger in scarlet, and the third was Adam o' the Dell. People called out, "Hey for Gilbert o' the Red Cap!" or "Ho for Adam o' the Dell!" No one shouted for the stranger in scarlet.

Gilbert shot first. His arrow flew straight and struck just a finger's breadth from the center of the target. The crowd shouted, "Gilbert! Gilbert!" The sheriff clapped his hands, saying, "Now that was a fine shot!"

Next came the stranger in scarlet. He pulled his bowstring back and shot quickly. The arrow sped through the air and struck the target just barely closer to the center than Gilbert's arrow had.

The sheriff's jaw dropped. "By all the saints in Heaven! That was an amazing shot!"

Adam o' the Dell drew his bow carefully. His

arrow struck the target close beside the stranger's. Once more, all three men shot. Adam o' the Dell's arrow struck farthest from the center. Again, the stranger dressed in scarlet shot the best.

All the men took a short rest, and then Gilbert readied to shoot again. He aimed carefully, and his arrow struck the target almost exactly in the center.

"Well done, Gilbert!" shouted the sheriff. "I do believe the prize is yours. Now, ragged knave in scarlet, let's see you shoot better than that."

The stranger drew his bow, held it for a moment, and then let his arrow fly. It struck the very center of the target, so close to Gilbert's arrow that it knocked a feather from the shaft. No one said a word, and no one clapped. Each man stared into the face of his neighbor, amazed.

Adam o' the Dell shook his head and un-strung his bow. "I've shot my last arrow for the day. No one can shoot better than that stranger dressed in red."

The Sheriff of Nottingham hurried up with the golden arrow. "Here, good fellow. You have won your prize fairly. What is your name?"

"Men call me Jock o' Teviotdale," said the stranger in scarlet.

"By Our Lady, Jock, you are the best archer I have ever seen," said the sheriff. "I believe you are better than that coward Robin Hood. He didn't dare show his face here today. Will you join my service?"

"Nay, I will not," said the stranger. "No man in all merry England shall be my master."

Angered, the sheriff shouted, "Leave, now! I have a good mind to have you beaten for your mouth." He turned on his heel and stalked away.

That night, the men gathered in Sherwood Forest for a wonderful woodland feast. Robin took off his scarlet coat and his eye patch. "I'm truly confused about what to do," Robin said. "The sheriff called me a coward. How can

I let him know who won the golden arrow?"

"Never fear, master. Will Stutely and I will send a message to the sheriff," said Little John.

The next day, as the sheriff dined with his wife, a servant rushed into the room, carrying an arrow. Tied to the arrowhead was a scroll of paper. The sheriff opened it and read this message:

Heaven bless the sheriff today,
So say all in Sherwood.
For you did give the prize away
To the merry Robin Hood.

The sheriff clenched his fist and shouted, "Where did this come from?"

"Th-th-through the window, your worship," stammered the servant in fear.

"I'll hang that vile knave from the tallest tree in Sherwood!" the sheriff roared.

CHAPTER 3

The Rescue of Will Stutely

The Sheriff of Nottingham's anger grew in the days that followed. He had been so sure his trap would work. "I have tried law, and I have tried being sneaky," he said to himself. "Now I will use force."

Three hundred men marched into Sherwood Forest. Whoever captured Robin Hood would win a hundred pounds. For seven days, they searched, but they never saw a single man dressed in Lincoln green. Robin had learned of the sheriff's plan at the Blue Boar Inn.

At first, Robin thought about fighting. He knew that his men were better than the sheriff's, but he finally decided to hide until the danger had passed. "Once I slew a man," he told them. "I don't wish to do it again, because it is a heavy weight for a soul to bear. We will hide in Sherwood. None of us will be harmed, and we will harm no one."

For seven days and seven nights, Robin and his men hid. On the morning of the eighth day, he asked, "Who will go find out what the sheriff's men are doing now?"

A great shout went up, and each man waved his bow in the air. Robin's heart swelled with pride. "A brave bunch of fellows you are, but you cannot all go. I select Will Stutely because he is sly like an old fox."

Will disguised himself as a friar, putting the brown robes over his Lincoln green. To his side, hidden by the robes, he strapped a sharp broadsword. Then he walked to the Blue Boar

Inn. He knew the innkeeper would have news.

When Will reached the inn, some of the sheriff's men were there. Will didn't fear them. He walked in and sat down at a table. As he waited for the innkeeper, a friendly fat cat rubbed up against Will's leg. The cat pushed Will's robe up far enough that his green clothes showed from beneath his disguise.

Will pulled his robe down again quickly, but it was too late. One of the sheriff's men saw the flash of green. "Tell me, holy father," the man asked, "where do you go on this hot summer day?"

"I am a pilgrim to Canterbury town," Will answered.

The sheriff's man sneered. "Do all pilgrims wear Lincoln green beneath their robes? You are no friar. You are one of Robin Hood's men!"

Flashing his sword, the sheriff's man leapt on Will, striking him once. Will drew his own sword quickly, but it was too late. The sheriff's man had wounded him, and Will grew dizzy. The other men grabbed him by the knees and dragged him to the floor.

The innkeeper sent his daughter to Robin Hood with the news. "Will Stutely has been captured," she told Robin. "He will be hanged tomorrow."

"He will not be hanged tomorrow," Robin replied. "If he is, the sheriff will pay."

Robin blew his bugle, and his men came running. He told them the bad news. "We must take our bows and our swords and rescue him. I know that we should risk our lives for Will, as he risked his life for us."

Early the next morning, Robin and his men arrived at Nottingham town. They waited outside the town gates until afternoon. A crowd began to gather. Everyone knew that brave Will Stutely was to hang that day.

Finally, a cart rolled through the gates. On it

stood Will Stutely. The Sheriff of Nottingham rode alongside. Will looked around for the faces of his friends, but he could not see them. His heart sank like a stone in a pond.

"Give me a sword and let me defend myself," Will said to the sheriff. "I am already wounded, but I will fight you and your men until all my strength is gone."

The sheriff snorted. "You will have no sword. You are a criminal, and you will die a grim death."

"Then untie my hands," demanded Will. "I will defend myself with my bare fists."

"Say your prayers, vile knave," the sheriff barked. "You hang from the gallows tree this very hour."

Will gnashed his teeth and shouted, "You coward! If Robin Hood ever meets you, you will pay dearly. He scorns you, as all brave men do. Do you know that your name is a joke to every brave man?"

"Oh, I'm a joke to your master?" screamed the sheriff in rage. "I will tear you limb from limb after you are hanged!"

As the cart approached the gallows, Will Stutely could not contain his tears. He bowed his head to hide them from the crowd. When he raised his head again, his heart leapt. Though his sight was blurred, he could see his friends crowding close. Then he saw his master, Robin Hood. Will could barely contain his joy.

Little John jumped onto the cart and cut the ropes that bound Will's hands. The sheriff charged and swung his sword at Little John's head. John ducked and quickly flicked his own sword, forcing the sheriff to drop his. John tossed the sword to Will. "Here, Will, the sheriff has lent you his sword!"

The sheriff shouted at the guards, "Get them!" Then an arrow whistled within an inch of his head. The frightened guards began to retreat.

The sheriff yelled at his men to hold, then ran himself.

"Oh, stay," Will called out. He turned to Little John and thanked him. "I didn't think that I would see you this day, or any other, before we met in Heaven. You are my true friend."

Though no one died that day, many of the sheriff's men had been injured. That frightened the sheriff. "These men fear nothing," he thought. "I would sooner lose my office than my life, so I will leave them alone."

CHAPTER 4

Robin Hood Plays Butcher

࠷

Robin Hood and his men did not leave Sherwood Forest for one whole year after rescuing Will Stutely. Whenever they caught a wealthy priest or landlord on the road through Sherwood, they took him to their place under the Greenwood Tree. There they held a great feast for the man they had captured. After the meal they made him pay, often with all the money he carried.

One morning, bored, Robin went looking for adventure. Reaching the edge of the forest, he spied a butcher, his horse-drawn cart full of meat. The butcher whistled merrily as he drove along.

"Hello, good friend," Robin said. "You certainly seem happy."

The butcher replied, "Yes, it's true. I am. I'm healthy, and it's a beautiful day. I love the prettiest lass in all Nottinghamshire, and I'm to marry her in Locksley town next Thursday."

"I was born and bred in Locksley town myself," said Robin. "I know it well. Where are you going this fine morning?"

"I am going to Nottingham town to sell my beef and mutton," said the butcher. "Who are you that comes from Locksley town?"

Robin smiled and bowed. "Call me Robin Hood."

"By God, I know the name well," exclaimed the butcher. "Please don't take anything from me. I am an honest man. I have harmed no one."

Robin Hood laughed. "I wouldn't take a

penny from an honest man such as yourself, especially one who hails from Locksley town! But tell me, what price would you ask for your cart, horse, and meat?"

"Hmmmn." The butcher thought for a moment. "The cart, horse, and meat are worth four pounds altogether."

Robin reached into his pouch and pulled out six pounds. "I would like to buy your cart and be a butcher for one day. Will you sell it to me?"

"May all the saints bless you!" cried the butcher. He jumped down from the cart and grabbed for the money Robin waved in front of him.

Robin laughed loudly. "Now get back to your lass and give her a kiss for me." Leaping into the driver's seat, he slapped the reins, and the horse trotted off through the forest.

When he reached the Nottingham market, Robin set up his stall among the other butchers.

Clanging his cleaver and a knife together, he began to sing:

> *Come ye lasses, come ye dames,*
> *Buy your meat from me.*
> *For three pennies' worth of meat I sell*
> *For the charge of one penny.*

When he finished his song, Robin called out, "Now, who will buy? Three pennies' worth of meat I sell to a fat friar for six pennies because I don't want his business. To lovely women, I sell three pennies' worth of meat for one penny. I like *their* business. To the lovely girl who likes a good butcher, I charge nothing but a kiss because I like her business best of all!"

A laughing crowd gathered. The meat was of the finest quality, and for the dames and girls of Nottingham town, the prices were excellent. Robin charged a widow or a poor woman noth-

ing at all. If a fair young lass came to Robin's stall, he charged only a kiss.

Some onlookers thought he was a thief who had stolen the cart and meat. But a thief would not give the meat away. Finally, everyone decided that Robin must be a rich man's son who thought giving away his money was fun.

Curious, some of the other butchers walked over to Robin's stall. "Come, brother, dine with us," they invited. "We are giving a great feast for the Sheriff of Nottingham at the Guild Hall."

"I will happily dine with you," said Robin with a tip of his cap.

The sheriff was eager to meet this butcher who gave meat away. Perhaps he could cheat him out of some money. He had seen Robin only twice, very briefly, and didn't recognize the young man when he entered the hall.

When dinner was served, the sheriff asked Robin to say grace. Robin prayed, "Now Heaven bless us and all the good meat and drink within this house, and may all butchers be as honest as I am."

Everyone laughed, especially the sheriff. "Surely this is some rich man's son," he thought. "Perhaps I can lighten his purse a bit." Patting Robin on the shoulder, the sheriff said, "You are a jolly young man."

"I know you love jolly young men," Robin replied. "Didn't you have a shooting match? And didn't you present Robin Hood with a bright golden arrow as the prize?"

The sheriff drew back and grew silent. Then Robin cried out, "I am paying for this feast. No one, not sheriff or butcher, shall reach for his purse tonight."

"You spend money so freely, young man," said the sheriff. "Surely you must have many acres of land and many horned beasts."

"I have more than five hundred horned beasts

I cannot sell," Robin said. "Otherwise, I would not have turned butcher."

The sheriff's eyes twinkled. "Perhaps I can help you. How much do you want for your beasts?"

"Five hundred pounds," said Robin.

"Well." The sheriff hesitated. "Five hundred pounds is a lot of money . . . I will give three hundred pounds."

"You old cheat," laughed Robin scornfully. "Five hundred horned beasts are worth seven hundred pounds. How could you swindle a poor youth like that? Don't look at me as though you just bit a sour egg. I will take your offer. My brothers and I enjoy a merry life, and a merry life requires money. I will take you to see my beasts this very day, but you must bring the money. I don't trust someone who drives so hard a bargain."

"I will bring the money. What is your name?" asked the sheriff.

"Men call me Robert o' Locksley," Robin replied.

"Robert o' Locksley, I will come today to buy your horned beasts. But mind you, you will not get the money until I get the beasts."

"Fair enough," agreed Robin.

Later that afternoon, he and the sheriff set out. When they had walked some distance, the sheriff saw the edge of Sherwood Forest. "May Heaven protect us from Robin Hood," he prayed.

"Oh, don't worry, good sheriff," said Robin. "I know Robin Hood well. You are in no more danger from him than you are from me."

The sheriff shuddered. "This young man seems too friendly with Robin Hood," he thought.

They traveled into the forest, down a winding

road. As they rounded a bend, a herd of deer pranced before them. Robin drew close to the sheriff and pointed. "Those are my horned beasts, sir. Are they not a sight to see?"

The sheriff stopped short. "I do not like your company," he said. "I wish to be away." The sheriff started to turn back, but Robin stopped him.

"Stay for a while," Robin said. "I would like you to meet my brothers." Then he put his bugle to his lips and blew three times. One hundred merry men ran up the path, Little John leading the way.

"How now, young master," said Little John.

"I have brought good company to feast with us," Robin told him. "Do you not recognize our good master, the Sheriff of Nottingham?"

The merry men raised their caps politely, and the sheriff grew very grim. He knew that Robin would take his three hundred pounds, and he feared for his life. Hadn't he tried to capture Robin Hood? Hadn't he tried to hang Will Stutely? Little John took the sheriff's arm gently but firmly and led him deeper into the forest.

Finally, they reached the glade where a broad oak spread its limbs. Beneath the Greenwood Tree, the men had laid out cushions of moss. Robin escorted the sheriff to a seat. No one had said anything about the money. "Perhaps he has forgotten," the sheriff thought.

Food arrived—fresh venison and fine breads—and the diners ate until they were full. As the moon began to rise, the sheriff yawned. "Thank you very much for a wonderful evening. But it grows late, and I must be leaving."

Robin shook the sheriff's hand. "Leave if you must, but you forget something. We run a merry inn here in the forest. Whoever comes as our guest must pay his bill."

The sheriff laughed hollowly. "Well, we have had a merry time. Even if you hadn't asked, I'd have been happy to give you twenty pounds for the food."

"Oh, no," said Robin seriously, "I would be ashamed to charge you less than three hundred pounds."

"Three hundred devils!" roared the sheriff. "Do you think your rotten food was worth three pounds, let alone three hundred?"

Robin said gravely, "Look around. There are men here who don't love you as I do. You will see Will Stutely, whom you tried to hang. Pay your bill without more ado, or it may be ill for you."

The sheriff grew pale. He bit his bottom lip, then reached for his money bag and gave it to Robin. Robin passed the bag to Little John and told him to count the money. The sheriff winced as if each coin were a drop of his own blood.

When John finished, Robin said, "Never before have we had such a generous guest! As it is very late, I will send one of my young men to guide you."

"No, heaven forbid," protested the sheriff. "I can find my own way."

"I will put you on the right track myself," Robin insisted. As they walked along, he warned the sheriff against trying to swindle young men. "Never buy a horse," Robin said, "without first looking it in the mouth."

CHAPTER 5

Little John Battles the Tanner of Blythe

୶

Little John had grown a bit fat over the winter, and Robin chided him frequently. "You've gained some softness around your belly," he teased one morning.

"I may be soft, Master Robin, but I'm not so soft that I can't still tumble a man from a forest bridge," John retorted. The merry men laughed. They remembered John and Robin's first meeting.

"That may be," chuckled Robin Hood, "but I am still the leader of this band, and I just remembered an errand I have for you. Some of the men need new clothes, but we are running low on Lincoln green and you need to buy cloth. I do believe the walk to Ancaster will do you good." Robin gave Little John money and sent him on his way.

Despite his size, Little John sometimes acted like a small boy. Robin Hood loved Little John, but he knew his right-hand man could be lazy at times. Robin followed at a distance to make sure Little John completed his errand in a timely fashion.

It was a beautiful day, with a few puffy clouds floating overhead. Little John was happy to be back in the forest again. As he ambled along, he saw a herd of deer trotting over a hill. Little John loved that sight. The law said the deer belonged to King Henry and that no man could hunt without the king's permission, but Little John felt that the deer belonged as much to Robin and the men as to the king.

As he approached the herd, Little John spied a man hiding by the side of the road. "Who goes there that hunts the king's deer?" he called out.

The stranger shouted back, "My name is Arthur a Bland, from Blythe. I'm a tanner by trade, not a poacher. I do no wrong."

This was only half true. Bland had no bow with him, but on many a day, he had hunted and killed the king's deer. Arthur a Bland enjoyed the taste of venison as much as any man.

Unconvinced, Little John said, "Well, you've got a criminal look about you. I do think you are a thief!"

"You lie through your teeth," declared Arthur a Bland.

"Is that so?" growled Little John. "I will give you a beating you will never forget! Now take up your staff, for I will not hit an unarmed man."

The two men came together slowly, circling

each other like angry dogs before a fight. Bland was not quite as tall as John, but he was an expert with the staff.

After a few moments, Little John struck. The blow clacked loudly against Bland's staff. Bland returned the blow, and John blocked it. Their mighty battle began.

Just then, Robin caught up with them. He heard the thunderous blows and crouched behind a tree to watch. "I would give three golden pounds to see this fellow beat Little John," Robin chuckled to himself. "Perhaps it would teach him a lesson for straying from his errand."

The two men fought on. Their feet wore out the earth beneath them, pushing it up in piles as they shoved one another up and down the forest floor with their staffs. "I have never seen anyone fight Little John like this before!" he said in amazement.

The contest continued for nearly an hour, but

then started to go badly for Little John. The extra weight he carried on his belly slowed him down, and he began to tire.

Finally, Little John saw his chance. Rearing back, he swung his staff as hard as he could. Though the blow was strong, Arthur a Bland wore a thick cowhide cap. He tumbled when John hit him on the head, but he did not lose his senses. As John moved to strike again, Bland regained his balance and hit John first. The blow knocked Little John to the forest floor, and his staff flew out of his hand. Arthur a Bland leapt forward and brought his staff down hard on Little John's ribs.

"Hold! Hold!" panted Little John. "Would you hit a man while he was down?"

"Why, yes, I would," Arthur a Bland replied. Then he struck again.

"Hold, I say!" cried Little John. "I give up!"

"Do you admit that I'm the better man?" Arthur a Bland demanded.

"Yes, yes I do," Little John said weakly.

Arthur a Bland relented. "Then you can go your way, and I'll go mine. You should be thankful that I am so merciful."

"You call that mercy?" asked Little John in disbelief. "Each of my ribs feels broken. I never thought I would meet the man who could do that to me."

Robin popped out from his hiding place. "I never thought I'd see it, either!" he laughed. "He knocked you down like a bottle off a wall!" Robin turned to Arthur a Bland. "What is your name, good fellow?"

"I am called Arthur a Bland. What is your name?"

"Ah! Arthur a Bland. You broke the crown of another friend of mine at the fair in Ely. This man you have just beaten is Little John. As for my name, men do call me Robin Hood."

"How now!" exclaimed Arthur a Bland. "You

are truly the great Robin Hood, and this is Little John? If I had known, I never would have raised my staff." Arthur a Bland bent down and began brushing off Little John's coat. "Let me help you, sir."

Little John rose from the ground as if his bones were made of glass. "I don't need your help. If you had not been wearing that leather cap, it would have been a very bad day for you."

Robin spoke again. "Arthur a Bland, would you like to join our band? You are one of the strongest men I've ever seen."

"Would I join your band?" exulted Arthur a Bland. "Why, I would like nothing better than to lead that merry life!"

Robin laughed, and the three men set out for Ancaster to buy the cloth of Lincoln green.

CHAPTER 6

The Stranger in Scarlet

Robin, Little John, and their new companion soon became thirsty. Stopping at a spring by the side of the road, the men drank from the clear, cool water.

As they rested, they saw a tall man walking lightly down the road. A broad velvet hat covered his long yellow hair, and he was dressed all in scarlet. In his hand, the man held a rose. Every few moments, he sniffed at it daintily.

"Have you ever seen such a fancy boy before?" chortled Robin.

"His clothes are much too pretty for a man," Arthur a Bland agreed, "but he is a big, broad, strong-looking fellow."

"Pah!" said Robin. "He would cry like a baby if he saw a mouse. I wonder who he is."

"Some baron's son," said Arthur a Bland. "His purse is probably filled with the money of honest workingmen."

Robin jumped to his feet. "Wait here while I teach this fellow a lesson. And you, Little John, pay attention."

The man saw Robin step into the middle of the road but did not change his pace. He continued to sniff at his rose as if he had not a care in the world. When the stranger was within a few feet, Robin raised his staff. "Hold! Hold! Stay where you are, fellow!"

In a soft voice, the man in red asked,

"Why should I hold? Why should I stay where I am?"

"Good friend," explained Robin, "I charge a toll on the road. It is a fee for carrying more money than the law allows. I will need to look inside your purse to see whether you have broken this law."

The tall stranger listened quietly. "You seem like a nice fellow, and I love to hear you talk, but I must be on my way."

"If you will give me your purse, I will let you be on your way," Robin replied.

"I am very sorry that I cannot do as you wish," the stranger said. "Let me go. I have done you no harm."

"I have told you, good fellow. You will go no farther until you do what I say!"

"Oh, good fellow, I am afraid I shall have to kill you," the stranger said quietly, drawing his sword.

"Put that down," Robin commanded. "My

stout staff will break it in two. I will not take advantage of you, so go cut yourself a proper staff."

The stranger said nothing. He replaced his sword in its scabbard and tossed aside his rose. Then he walked into the woods and chose a small tree. Arthur a Bland and Little John watched in wonder as the stranger grabbed the tree with both hands and pulled it out of the ground, roots and all.

"By the saints in Heaven!" exclaimed Arthur a Bland. "He pulled up that tree like a weed in a garden. I think our master stands a poor chance against this stranger in scarlet."

With his dagger, the stranger calmly trimmed the tree to the right size. He stepped to the middle of the road, where Robin stood waiting.

The two men fought furiously. The stranger was stronger than Robin, but Robin had more skill. A cloud of dust rose around them. Robin dodged the powerful blows of his opponent, but his own blows were blocked. Finally, the stranger struck at Robin with great force. Though Robin blocked the strike, he felt his staff bend. The stranger struck furiously, again and again, forcing Robin to the ground. "Hold! Hold!" he cried. "I say hold! I give up!"

Little John and Arthur a Bland rushed forward, shouting, "Hold! Hold!"

The stranger in red spun around to face them. "Well, if you two fellows are as strong as he is, I will have my hands full. But I will try to serve you as well."

"Stop!" bellowed Robin. "We will fight no more." He turned to Little John. "This is a very bad day for us. I do wonder whether my arm is broken."

Little John's eyes twinkled. "How now, good master. Here, let me dust off your coat. Let me help you get up."

Robin shook off Little John's aid and scrambled up. Turning to the stranger, Robin asked, "What is your name?"

"Gamwell," answered the stranger.

"Ha! Is that so?" said Robin. "I have kin with the same name. Where do you come from?"

"I hail from Maxwell town and come to find my uncle, whom men call Robin Hood," the stranger explained. "I wonder if you could direct me?"

Robin clapped his hands on Gamwell's shoulders. "Will Gamwell! It can be no other. Look at me, and tell me if you know me."

Young Gamwell looked deeply into Robin's eyes. "By the breath in my body, I do believe you are my own uncle Robin!"

CHAPTER 7

Robin Hood's Long-Lost Kinsman

Robin had not seen Will Gamwell for ten years, and the two men hugged joyfully. Before becoming an outlaw, Robin had taught the boy Will to use a bow and arrow. He had also taught him to fight with a staff—very well it seemed!

"I hope I didn't hurt you, Uncle Robin," apologized Will.

"My arm will tingle for a few days, but it will be fine," Robin replied. "My heart dropped when I saw you uproot that tree. You have become a very strong man. Tell me, what brings you to Sherwood Forest?"

"It is a long story," Will said sadly. "I hit a man who threatened my old father. I did not intend it, but the force of the blow killed the man. Now I have been charged with murder."

"I am very sorry to hear of your ill fortune, Will, but I am very glad that you will join our band," Robin comforted him. "You must have a new name because warrants for your arrest will be sworn out. Aha! Your clothes give me an idea! You shall be known as Will Scarlet."

Little John shook Will's hand. "Will Scarlet, I am very glad to meet you. My name is Little John. This is a new member of our band, Arthur a Bland. You will surely become famous, Will Scarlet. Many minstrels will sing about how you beat the stout Robin Hood in a fair fight with staffs."

"Let us say no more about that, Little John," warned Robin.

"Why, good master, I thought you liked a good laugh," said Little John. "Did you not tease me about a certain fatness of my limbs?"

"I will say no more about that, Little John. Let us keep this story among ourselves," Robin insisted.

"You also enjoyed it very much when our new friend Arthur a Bland got the better of me," teased Little John.

"A curse on you, Little John! I will say no more of it."

"Fair enough," agreed Little John. "I was blinded today. I did not see you take a beating from the young Will Scarlet. Any man who says I did will get a beating from me."

"Today I have gained the strongest men in all of Nottinghamshire," Robin declared. "We can go to Ancaster another day. Now let us return to the Greenwood Tree. Perhaps rest will mellow the pain I feel in my bones and joints."

CHAPTER 8

Robin Hood Befriends Allan a Dale

᷍

Two days after Will Scarlet and Arthur a Bland donned the Lincoln green, Robin took Will Stutely aside. "Will, lead these new lads to the highway. Teach them how Robin Hood and his men find paying guests for their merry feasts."

Will Stutely grinned. "I will be happy to take these fellows out on such a hunt." The party gathered and set forth. Finding a comfortable grassy place by the highway, the men sat down and waited. Fair damsels and stout shepherds strolled past. A tinker clattered down the road with his wares. Women taking eggs to market bustled along, but the men saw no one worth robbing. As the sun began to set, the shadows grew long.

"What bad luck," grumbled Will Stutely. "If I had gone on an innocent errand, I would have seen fat rich men and spoiled priests by the dozen. Now we are here to take such a guest back to the Greenwood Tree, and we see no one. Come, good fellows, let us return to the forest."

They had walked for a while when Will Stutely put up his hand. "Hold, lads, I hear something." They all stopped.

"We must look into this," said Will Scarlet. "Someone is in trouble."

"I'm not so sure about that," said Will Stutely. "That is a man's voice. I say a man should take care of his own troubles."

"That's a terrible way to think," said Will Scarlet. "Stay here if you like, but I'm going to see what's wrong."

"I did not say that I wouldn't go. I merely recommended caution," Will Stutely retorted. He began to walk toward the sound, and the others followed. The woods opened onto a pool of water, fed by a chattering brook. A young man sat at the edge of the pool, crying softly. On the tree above him hung a fine harp of polished wood. By his side lay a bow and a quiver of arrows.

"Hello!" shouted Will Stutely. "Who weeps there, killing the green grass with his flow of salt tears?"

The young stranger sprang to his feet, grabbed his bow, and fitted an arrow against the string.

"Hold, fellow," Will Stutely warned, "we are not going to harm you. Put down that bow and wipe your eyes. I hate to see a big strong fellow sniveling like a little girl over a dead kitten."

"I know that young man," Arthur a Bland said. "He is a famous minstrel in these parts. I saw him but a week ago. He sang like a bird and skipped like a yearling doe."

"Pay no attention to these fellows," urged Will Scarlet. "They are rough, but they mean well. Come with us. Perhaps we can help solve your problems, whatever they are."

The young stranger took his harp down from the tree and walked sadly alongside the men. He kept his head low and said nothing.

As the moon rose above the treetops, they came to the glade where the Greenwood Tree stood. A great feast was being readied for some lucky guest. Thick steaks of venison sizzled over the fire, and a mouthwatering smell drifted through the forest.

Robin greeted the young stranger. "Good evening, fair friend. Have you come to feast with me today?"

The young man looked around with wide

eyes. "I think I know where I am. Are you the great Robin Hood?"

Robin laughed. "Bull's-eye! Because you know me, you also know that you must pay for this evening's feast. I trust you have a full purse, fair stranger."

"I have nothing but a sixpence, broken in half," the young stranger confessed. "My one true love has the other half of the coin. She wears it on a silken thread around her neck."

Robin Hood spoke sharply to Will Stutely. "Is this the kind of guest you think will fill our purse?"

"No, good master," Will answered. "Will Scarlet brought him along. Nevertheless, I think this boy may offer us an opportunity to do some good."

Will Scarlet told Robin how they had found the lad crying by the side of the pool. They believed he was in some trouble.

Robin put his hands on the boy's shoulders and looked him in the eye. "You have got a good face, an honest and kind face." The young man's eyes filled with tears. "Don't cry, lad. I'm sure your troubles can be fixed. What is your name?"

"Allan a Dale, sir," the boy murmured.

"Are you not the young minstrel I have been hearing about?" asked Robin.

"Yes, sir, that is me," replied Allan a Dale.

"Come eat with me and tell me your problems," Robin said. "You will feel better if you talk."

CHAPTER 9

Allan a Dale's Plight

As Robin and Allan a Dale ate, the young minstrel told his story. At first, his words came slowly. When he saw that Robin Hood and his men were listening carefully, the words began to tumble forth.

Allan a Dale traveled through the countryside, singing his songs and playing his harp. One day, he stopped at a farmhouse, where he sang for the farmer and his fair daughter, Ellen. The girl was so beautiful that Allan a Dale returned and watched for her. At first, he was shy. As his feelings grew, he became bold enough to walk with Ellen. They sat on a riverbank, and he told her she was his one true love. She confessed that she loved him, too. Allan a Dale broke a sixpence and gave Ellen half of the coin to wear around her neck.

When the farmer learned that his daughter was in love with Allan a Dale, he became very angry. He had already promised her to Sir Stephen of Trent, a very old knight. But Ellen did not love the knight. Allan had learned that very morning that Ellen would marry Sir Stephen in two days.

"I have a good mind to pummel Sir Stephen!" said Little John. "An old man like that has no right to marry such a young girl."

"Are you certain she will marry him?" asked Robin.

"She will do as her father tells her, but she will die of heartbreak," Allan mourned.

Robin thought somberly for a moment, and then his eyes brightened. "I think I have a plan. Tell me, Allan, do you think fair Ellen would marry you if we brought her before a priest and got her father's blessing?"

"Of course she would," said Allan a Dale.

"Then my plan should work. We need only a priest," Robin said. "I know none around here with any great love for me, though. That's the sticking point."

Will Scarlet spoke up. "I know a priest who would surely perform the ceremony. He is the Curtal Friar of Fountains Abbey, not far from here."

"Then we shall go see him tomorrow," decided Robin. "Don't worry, Allan. We have your troubles in hand."

Allan a Dale's tears had dried by then. He had heard many tales of how Robin Hood helped people and wanted to believe that Robin could help him. Allan's spirits rose, and he picked up his harp. His voice was so sweet that the men asked Allan to sing one song after another, late into the night. Finally, Robin called an end to the evening.

"Tomorrow we must find the Curtal Friar of Fountains Abbey. We need to go early if we are to help young Allan," Robin announced. Following his lead, everyone retired for some much-needed rest.

CHAPTER 10

Robin Hood Finds the Curtal Friar

The next morning, Robin and the merry men sprang out of bed at first light. They had to find the Curtal Friar of Fountains Abbey quickly if they hoped to stop Ellen's wedding.

Will Scarlet knew the way to the abbey, so he led the others. The path took them through woods they had never traveled. Just after noon, they reached a broad, fast-flowing river. "In a bit, we will come to a shallow place in the river," Will said. "We can wade across there."

Robin shook his head. "I think I should go the

rest of the way alone. If I have any trouble, I will blow my bugle three times."

About ten minutes after leaving his men, Robin suddenly stopped and listened for a moment. "That's strange. It seems I am hearing two voices, yet they sound almost the same. What is going on?" he wondered.

Peering through the trees, Robin saw a fat friar sitting on the riverbank. He was a jolly-looking fellow with a thick neck and bright red cheeks. Between his legs sat a big meat pie. In one hand, he held a bottle. The other hand clutched a crust of pie.

"Oh, good fellow," the friar said, "you are the best friend I could ever have." Then a different voice responded. "Why thank you, brother. I do appreciate your kindness." The friar replied in the first voice, "Why thank *you*, brother. You must try this pie."

Robin held in his laughter.

When the friar finished his meal, he rubbed his hands together, then said, "Good friend, I have enjoyed this meal. I would like it so very much if you would sing a bit for me." The second voice said, "I would love to, but I won't sing alone. Will you join me?" The friar nodded and began to sing in a strong, deep voice.

Robin chuckled quietly. He knew the tune, so he began to sing along. Startled, the friar struggled clumsily to his feet. He drew his broadsword from its scabbard and cried out, "Show yourself, and I'll carve you like a Sunday roast beef!"

Robin emerged from his hiding place. "Oh, good brother, put your sword away. Haven't we shared a song? Why should we fight? I'll tell you, good friend, the song has left me parched. Have you any drink to wash my throat?"

The friar lowered his sword glumly. "You seem to be very comfortable barging in where you are not invited. But I am a Christian and cannot refuse drink to a thirsty man." He held out the bottle.

Robin grabbed it, threw his head back, and drank until the bottle was empty. The friar snatched the bottle back and peered inside. He turned the bottle upside down and shook it, but nothing came out. Then he pursed his lips and glared.

Ignoring the look, Robin asked, "Do you know of a certain one who goes by the name of Curtal Friar of Fountains Abbey?"

"Yea, a bit," replied the friar.

"Well then, good father or friar, or whatever you are," said Robin, "I would like to know whether he will be found on this side of the river or the other."

"I advise you to set foot on that side of the river and find out for yourself," snapped the friar.

"Well, good friar, as you can see, my clothes are of fine quality," Robin explained. "I don't want to get them wet. You have broad, strong shoulders. Would you mind carrying me across?"

The friar turned as red as an apple. "You little runt!" he shouted. "Do you dare ask that I carry you across?" Then the anger left his face, and his eyes twinkled once more. "But why should I not? Climb up on my back. I will carry you safely across the river."

The friar bent down, and then suddenly straightened up again. "I think you will get your weapon wet, young master. Let me tuck your sword under my arm to keep it dry."

"No, good father. I wouldn't have you carry any more," protested Robin.

"Don't you think that the good Saint Christopher would have carried it for you? Now give your weapon to me."

Robin unbuckled his sword and climbed up on the friar's back. The strong friar easily carried Robin across the stream. When they reached the other side, Robin jumped down. "Please give me my sword, quickly. I am in a hurry."

The friar smiled. "You have business on *this* side of the river. But I have my own business, young master. My business is on the *other* side. I am no longer a young man. I'm sure that if I wade through the river once more, I will develop cricks and pains in my back," he wheedled. "Please, do me the favor of carrying me across."

Robin looked up and down the river. "You sneak," he sputtered.

"Hurry, young man," warned the friar, "unless you want to feel the nip of steel against your flesh."

"You win," Robin said coldly. "I will carry you. Give me my sword. I won't use it against you."

The friar eyed Robin warily. "Here is your skewer. Now quickly, haul me across the river."

Robin bent down. The friar leapt onto his back, and Robin stepped into the flowing stream.

The friar was much fatter than Robin, so Robin's load across the river was much greater than the friar's had been. The friar dug his heels into Robin's sides as if he were a donkey.

Robin didn't know the way as well as the friar, so he stumbled every few steps. At every stumble, however, Robin reached up and loosened the friar's sword belt. When they reached the opposite side, Robin pulled the belt off. The friar did not feel it and jumped down. Now Robin held the friar's sword as well as his own.

The friar looked at Robin intently. "I didn't take you for such a clever lad. You have gotten the better of me. Give me my sword, and I will carry you back to the other side."

Robin returned the sword belt, and the friar buckled it securely around his waist. Robin merrily jumped up on the friar's back and prodded the friar along with his heels, as the friar had done to him. When they reached the middle of the river, the friar stopped to rest for a moment. Suddenly, he stood upright and flipped Robin over his back. "There," crowed the friar, "let *that* cool your hot spirit!"

Robin landed in the cold water with a great splash. Stumbling to his feet, he coughed water from his nose and mouth. "I will slice you to bits this day, villain," Robin swore. He scampered up the riverbank, drew his sword, planted his feet, and waited.

The friar still stood in the middle of the river.

"Don't worry, I will join you shortly. Then I will make you beg for mercy."

Slowly, the friar hauled himself up the bank and drew his own sword. The two men came together with a furious clash. The clang of metal rang through the forest for an hour, but neither man wounded the other. They stopped to rest, hands on their knees, panting heavily. Looking at each other, they shook their heads. Then they fought again. At last, Robin said, "Hold your hand, good fellow."

Weary, both men lowered their swords. The friar thought it would be a terrible thing to wound so strong an opponent. Robin thought the same.

"Let me do one thing," Robin gasped.

"What would that be?" wheezed the friar.

"Let me blow on this horn three times."

"I think you have a trick up your sleeve," the friar said, breathing hard. "But I don't fear you.

I will let you blow on your horn three times, if you will let me blow my whistle."

"Agreed," said Robin, "but I will go first." He raised the bugle and blew three long, clear blasts. A moment later, Robin's companions came running. Their bows were drawn, ready to shoot.

"So that's your trick!" cried the friar. "Well, this is mine." He blew his little silver whistle. A sharp, high note rang out. Suddenly, four fierce hounds burst from the thicket. "Get 'em, Sweet Lips! Bell Throat, Beauty, Fang, get 'em!" the friar shouted.

The dogs charged. Each man, except for Will Scarlet, drew back an arrow and let it fly. The dogs leapt out of the way. As the arrows whistled past, the dogs snatched them from the air and snapped them in their dripping jaws. Then the dogs charged again. Will Scarlet stepped toward them with his hand out, and they stopped. As he patted their heads, they lapped at his palms like puppies.

"Are you a wizard that you can turn these wolves into lambs?" wondered the friar. He looked carefully at Will's face. "Can I trust my eyes? What does it mean that I see young Will Gamwell in such poor company?"

"Hello, Tuck," Will greeted him. "My name is no longer Gamwell. Men call me Will Scarlet now. This is my good uncle, Robin Hood. I live with him in Sherwood Forest."

The friar's jaw dropped. He held out his hand. "I have heard your name often, good master. I never thought to meet you in battle. Please forgive me. Now I know why you were so stout an opponent." The friar turned back to Will Scarlet. "How is it that you live in Sherwood now?"

"Have you not heard about the events that befell me?" asked Will.

The friar shook his head grimly. "Yes, I have. It's a great shame that a gentleman should be forced to hide because of an accident."

Robin Hood was growing impatient. "We don't have much time. I've yet to find this Curtal Friar."

Will Scarlet started to laugh. He looked at Robin and then at the friar. "Good uncle, you don't have to go far. He's standing right beside you."

Robin turned on the friar. "You? You're the man I've been looking for all day?"

"Truly," said the friar. "Some do call me the Curtal Friar of the Fountain Dale. Others call me the Abbot of Fountains Abbey as a joke. Still others call me simple Friar Tuck."

"I like the last name best," said Robin. "Why didn't you tell me who you are, instead of sending me on a wild goose chase?"

"You did not ask, good master," said Friar Tuck meekly. "What do you desire from me?"

Robin glanced at the sun. "The day is getting late, and we can't waste any more time. Come with us to Sherwood, and I will tell you along the way." He whistled for the dogs, which bounded along with them.

They departed on the trip back to Sherwood, all six men with the dogs following at their heels. It was long past nightfall by the time they reached the Greenwood.

CHAPTER 11

Robin Hood Arranges the Marriage of Two Lovers

∽

After arriving at the Greenwood Tree, Robin and his men set to work. Robin chose twenty strong men and gave Little John two bags of golden pounds. "This is two hundred pounds of my own money. Be ready to give it to me when I ask."

Then Robin went to the store of costumes the merry men kept. Choosing some brightly colored clothes, he designed his disguise. He would go to the wedding as a festive minstrel. Robin picked up a harp and strummed it a few times.

"Good master, I didn't know you played the harp," said Little John. Robin couldn't play at all, but for his plan that didn't matter.

Early on the morning of Ellen's wedding day, Robin led his men, along with Allan a Dale and Friar Tuck, to the church. They hid behind the wall across the road, where they waited the whole morning. David of Duncaster peeked above the stones every few minutes to see whether anyone was near. Finally, he saw an old priest heading toward the door.

Robin turned to Friar Tuck. "Go, good brother. Talk to that priest and get yourself into the church."

Friar Tuck clambered over the wall. The old priest was trying to open the door to the church, but he couldn't turn the heavy key in the lock.

"Let me help you with that, brother." Tuck took the key and easily opened the door. "I am a poor hermit from Fountains Abbey. I have come because I hear there is a fine wedding to be held in this church today. May I enter?"

"I don't give a fig what you do," the old priest muttered. "Go, enter."

When Friar Tuck stepped through the entrance, Robin sauntered up to the door and sat down. Soon, a group of men on horseback drew near. With them rode the Bishop of Hereford, one of the richest bishops in all of England.

Robin grew angry at the sight of the bishop's fine silk robes and gold chains. He thought it wrong that a man of God should dress in such fancy clothes and jewelry.

"Hello there," the bishop called. "Who are you that struts about in such colorful feathers?"

"I am a harper from the North Country," answered Robin. "I can touch the strings like no man in all of England. If you let me play for this wedding, I promise that the bride will love her man as long as they both live."

The bishop was the cousin of Sir Stephen of Trent. He knew very well that Sir Stephen loved Ellen with all his heart. He also knew that Sir Stephen was far too old for Ellen and that she didn't love him. "Is it true?" asked the bishop. "If you can play as well as you say you can, I will give you anything you ask."

Just then, they heard the sound of horses. The bishop turned to greet the wedding party riding toward the church.

Robin spotted Sir Stephen, dressed all in silk. Beside Sir Stephen rode Ellen's father, Edward the farmer. Two horses pulled Ellen's carriage, and six men-at-arms followed.

When the carriage reached the door of the church, Ellen stepped out. Robin had never seen a more beautiful girl. Her skin was pale and smooth, but she carried herself like a wilting flower. Anyone could see that this was not a happy day for her.

A few minutes later, the wedding party gathered in the church. Ellen looked around fearfully. The bishop was about to begin the ceremony when Robin trotted up to the altar.

"Let me look at the lass," Robin said. He took her hands and studied her face. "Look here, her cheeks are pale as snow, not bright red with the happiness one should see on a young bride. This is not a fit wedding. Sir Stephen, you are too old and she is too young. You are not her one true love."

Everyone in the church looked at Robin in amazement. As they stood in stunned silence, Robin blew his horn three times. Little John and Will Stutely leapt to the front of the church and drew their swords.

Ellen's father strode to the altar. He would have dragged his daughter away, but Little John said, "Stand back, old man. You're a hobbled horse today."

"Down with the villains," cried Sir Stephen.

As his men-at-arms drew their swords, the door of the church was flung open. Steel flashed in the light. Allan a Dale, leading eighteen of Robin's men, carried Robin's bow in his hands. He handed it to Robin and dropped to one knee.

Ellen's father bellowed, "Is it Allan a Dale who has ruined this day?"

"No," Robin answered. "*I* have done all this to save this day from ruination. I don't care who knows it. My name is Robin Hood."

Everyone in the church fell silent. The bishop closed his book and murmured, "Heaven protect us from this evil man."

"I mean you no harm," Robin assured him. "But Allan a Dale is Ellen's one true love. She shall marry him, or pain will come to all of you."

Ellen's father boomed out. "No! I am her father! I say she shall marry Sir Stephen and no one else!"

Sir Stephen faced Ellen's father. "No, good

fellow. You may take your daughter back. I would not marry her after today's doings for all the wealth in England. I do love her, as old as I am. But I did not know that she loves this fellow." Then he turned to Ellen. "Maiden, if you would rather marry a minstrel than a high-born knight, that is your choice." His men-at-arms gathered around him as he walked proudly out of the church.

"Well," the Bishop of Hereford announced, "since I now have no business here, I too will depart."

Robin placed his hand on the bishop's chest. "Stay, good bishop, for I have something to say." The bishop's face fell. He knew that Robin would not let him go.

"Bless your daughter's marriage to Allan a Dale, and all will be well," Robin urged Ellen's father. "Little John, hand me the bags of gold. Look, farmer. Here are two hundred bright golden angels. Give your blessing, and I will count them out to you."

Edward stared at the ground, his brow wrinkling. He saw plainly that Ellen would now marry Allan a Dale no matter what. "I had thought to make a lady of her," Edward said. "I will have nothing more to do with her if she marries this man, but I will give my blessing when she is wed."

The old priest shook his head. "It may not be," he said stubbornly. "There is no priest here who will marry them."

"What did you say?" roared Friar Tuck from the organ loft. "No priest? I am as holy a man as you, seven days a week!"

After the ceremony, Robin turned to the Bishop of Hereford. "I promised your lordship I could make sure that the bride loved the man she married.

There is the bride, and she loves her groom. You promised *me* that you would give me whatever I asked if I accomplished this feat. I want the golden chain that hangs around your neck so that I may give it to the fair Ellen as a wedding present."

The bishop turned red with rage. He slowly lifted the chain from his neck and handed it to Robin. Robin draped the chain around Ellen's neck. It glittered about her shoulders.

"I thank you for your handsome gift," Robin told the bishop. "Truly, you look better without it. Please come soon to Sherwood Forest. We will honor you with a feast such as you have never had in your whole life."

"Heaven forfend!" prayed the bishop. He knew very well that Robin's guests paid for feasts with all the money they carried.

CHAPTER 12

Robin Hood Aids a Sorrowful Knight

⸎

Autumn came quickly to Sherwood Forest. After the joy of Allan a Dale's wedding, the spring and summer sped past. Robin woke up one bright October morning and realized that winter was near. The men of Sherwood Forest had entertained no guests for several weeks. He said to Little John, "Winter is coming, friend, and our money is running low. We had better find ourselves some wealthy dinner guests before the freezing wind blows."

Everyone knows that you catch more fish

with two hooks than with one. Robin told Little John to choose a group of men and search to the west for a rich guest. Will Scarlet, Allan a Dale, and Midge the miller's son joined Robin, and they set out toward the east.

Robin and his men walked for most of the morning. When they found a shady, comfortable spot by the side of the road, they sat down to wait. Many honest, hardworking people passed by, but no rich landlords or false friars traveled among them. The men carried lunches of cold meat and bread. They ate quietly, enjoying the gentle fall breeze.

The afternoon wore on. As the men got ready to return to Sherwood, a tall knight rode into view. His clothes were plain but well made. He wore no gold chain or jeweled rings, as most knights did. The knight rode slowly, his head hung low.

"There is a very sorrowful-looking knight,"

Robin observed. "But even if he is sad, his clothes look rich. Stay here, men, while I look into the matter."

Robin stepped out onto the road when the knight drew close. "Hold, sir knight. Please wait here a moment."

"Who are you to stop men on our king's highway?" asked the knight.

"That is a hard question," replied Robin. "Some men call me a good, honest fellow. Others call me a vile thief. Your regard for me depends entirely on your own self. My name is Robin Hood."

"Truly, good Robin," said the knight, smiling, "you have a clever way of talking. As for my regard, I say it is very favorable. I hear much good of you and little bad. What do you want from me?"

"Sir knight, if you follow me into Sherwood, we will give you a feast such as you have never had before."

The sad knight shook his head slowly. "You are kind, but I think you will find me a heavy-hearted and sorrowful guest. Let me pass."

"No," said Robin. "We keep a type of inn here. All our guests have a very merry time, but they must pay for their food and entertainment."

"I understand what you're saying," said the knight, "but I am not your man. I have no money with me."

"Is it true?" asked Robin. "I want to believe you, but there are men like you whose word is not to be trusted." He whistled, and his men emerged from hiding. "These are my merry men. They share in my fortune and loss, my happiness and my sorrow. Please tell me, good knight, what money *do* you have?"

The knight did not speak for a few minutes. His cheeks grew red. "I don't know why I feel shame, but I do. I tell you the truth, friend, when I say that my purse contains six shillings. That is all the money that I, Sir Richard of the Lea, have in the whole world."

Robin listened quietly. "You give me your knightly word that is all the money you have?"

"Yes," answered Sir Richard. "I do pledge my most solemn word, as a true knight. Here is my purse. You may search it yourselves."

"Keep your purse, Sir Richard," said Robin. "The proud I strive to bring low. Those who walk in sorrow, I aim to help if I can. Sir Richard, come with us to Sherwood."

"I know you mean to be kind," said Sir Richard, "but I doubt that you can help me with my troubles. Nevertheless, I shall go."

"Sir knight," Robin said kindly, "I don't mean to bother you, but could you tell me what troubles you so?"

"Truly, Robin, I see no reason why I should not," replied Sir Richard. "My castle and lands are mortgaged for a debt I owe. Three days from now, the Prior of Emmett will sell all if I do not pay the money."

"How did this happen?" asked Robin.

"I have a twenty-year-old son. Already he is a knight. Last year, he went to the jousts at Chester and unhorsed all the men he rode against. Finally, he faced a great knight, Sir Walter of Lancaster. My son's lance knocked Sir Walter from his horse. The tragedy is that a splinter from the lance slipped through his helmet. The splinter pierced Sir Walter's eye, and he died. His relatives had many friends in the court. I was able to save my son from the dungeon only by paying a ransom of six hundred pounds in gold. Because I didn't have the money, I mortgaged my lands to the Prior of Emmett. He drove a hard bargain in my hour of need."

"How much money do you owe?" asked Robin.

"Only four hundred pounds," Sir Richard replied.

"Only four hundred pounds!" exclaimed Will Scarlet. "Don't you have friends who can help you?"

"When I was rich, I had many friends who boasted of their love for me," the knight responded. "They are nowhere to be found now."

"You say you have no friends, Sir Richard," Robin said. "I make no boast, but I may be able to help you yet."

CHAPTER 13

The Bishop "Helps" Robin and Sir Richard

 ∽

When the party reached the Greenwood Tree, they saw that Little John's men had captured the Bishop of Hereford and his attendants. Robin saw pack horses loaded with goods. He also saw that one horse carried a big locked wooden box. Robin's eyes gleamed. He knew such a box held treasure.

The bishop spotted Robin and charged toward him like a bull. Robin smiled. "Hello, your holiness! I will be with you in a moment. Don't worry, there's not another man in all England I'd rather speak with."

The bishop's face swelled with rage. "Is this the way you and your ragtag band treat a man so high in the church as I?" he shouted. "These friars and I were traveling peacefully down the road when up comes a great strapping fellow, a full seven feet high. He's with eighty men, and they demand that we stop. He called me fat priest, man-eating bishop, and whatnot as if I were no more than a beggar!"

Robin said, "Alas, my lord, you have truly been ill treated by my band. Little John, come here for a moment."

Little John came forward, pretending to be ashamed, like a child caught stealing sweets.

Robin said to the bishop, "Is this the man who spoke so boldly to your lordship?"

"Yes it is," fumed the bishop. "He's an evil fellow."

Robin turned to Little John. "Little John, did you call his lordship a fat priest?"

"Yes, I did," Little John said sorrowfully.

"And a man-eating bishop?"

"Yes," replied Little John, even more sorrow-fully.

"Alas, then these things must be true," concluded Robin. "Little John is an honest man, and I know he would not lie to a bishop!"

The bishop's blood boiled so hotly that his face turned cherry red from his scalp to his chin, but he swallowed his words.

"Now, my good bishop, we are rough fellows," said Robin Hood. "But we are not so rough as you might believe. All are equal here in the Greenwood, and all who come to dine with us must share our merry life. So too must you."

While some of the men ran to prepare the meal, others brought out staffs and longbows. Soft animal pelts were laid out on the ground as seats for the guests. Robin seated Sir Richard of the Lea next to the Bishop of Hereford.

When everyone was comfortable, some men
hung a wreath of green branches from a distant
tree. The men each aimed three arrows at the
wreath. Although it was just four palms wide,
only two arrows missed the ring. "I have never
seen such shooting!" the bishop exclaimed.
"Robin Hood, I have often heard of your skill.
Will you show me a sample?"

Robin jumped lightly to his feet. From a wil-
low tree, he cut a slim stick and whittled one end
to a point. He walked off in the distance, stuck the
sharpened stick into the ground, and then
returned to where the bishop sat. Robin took up
his bow and chose a very straight arrow with
flawless feathers. He placed the notched end of
the arrow over the string of his bow, drew back
quickly, and shot. An instant later, a great shout
arose. Robin's arrow had split the narrow stick
and lodged halfway through it! The bishop was
amazed. The merry men raised a cheer for

Robin Hood. They were proud of his skill.

Soon great platters of savory meats appeared. After everyone had eaten his fill, Robin called for silence. When everyone hushed, he spoke.

"I have a story to tell, so listen to what I say." Then Robin Hood repeated Sir Richard's sad tale. "Now Sir Richard will surely lose his castle and his lands to the Prior of Emmett," Robin said at the end. He looked at the bishop. "Is that the way for a servant of God to behave?" The bishop stared at the ground, afraid to meet anyone's eye.

"You are the richest bishop in all of England," Robin cajoled. "Can you help this needy brother?"

The bishop said nothing.

Robin turned to Little John. "Get the bundles that the bishop and his men carried."

Little John and Will Stutely laid the bundles out on the grass in front of everyone. Little John handed Robin a list of goods. Robin asked Will

Scarlet to read the list aloud so everyone could hear. Some items, such as candles for the Chapel of St. Thomas, Robin let the bishop keep. Other items, such as bundles of silk, would be sold for charity. Finally, they came to the last item on the list. Will Scarlet read, "A box belonging to the Lord Bishop of Hereford."

The bishop shuddered as if he had a chill.

"Do you have a key for this box?" asked Robin.

The bishop shook his head.

Robin told Will Scarlet to break the lock. Will drew his sword and brought it down heavily on the box. Sparks flew, and the front of the box cracked open. Heavy gold coins poured out like water from a broken barrel.

Robin told Will Scarlet, Little John, and Allan a Dale to count the money. They counted for a long time while everyone waited.

Finally, Will called out, "Fifteen hundred golden pounds."

"My lord bishop," Robin declared, "I will let you keep one-third of the money. Five hundred pounds you will pay for this evening's entertainment. Another five hunderd pounds goes to the charity of my choosing."

Robin Hood beckoned to Sir Richard. "Sir Richard, you will take the five hundred pounds and pay your debt to the Prior of Emmett. It seems right that a surplus of church money should be used to aid you."

"I thank you, friend, for what you do for me," said Sir Richard gratefully, "but I cannot take this money as a gift. It is a loan, and I will repay it either to you or the bishop one year and one day from now. I give my knightly word."

"Truly, sir knight, I do not understand why you insist, but it will be as you wish," Robin replied. "Perhaps you should bring the money to me. I believe I will make better use of it than the bishop would."

Sir Richard rose from his seat. "I cannot stay later, good friends. My lady will be anxious if I do not return home soon, so I crave to depart."

"We cannot let you go home unattended, without men-at-arms," Robin said.

Little John leapt to his feet. "Good master, let me choose twenty men. We will arm ourselves and accompany Sir Richard until he can get retainers of his own."

Robin Hood agreed. "So it will be done."

Will Scarlet said, "We should give Sir Richard a gold chain to hang from his neck and golden spurs."

"That too will be done."

Then Will Stutely called out, "Let us give Sir Richard a bale of velvet and that roll of golden silk as a proper gift for his lady."

Everyone cheered, and Robin laughed. "You have spoken well, Will Stutely. It will be done."

Sir Richard of the Lea felt tears of gratitude rising in his eyes. "Good friends, I shall always remember your kindness. If ever you are in trouble, you may come to the Castle of the Lea. Its walls may be battered to the ground before harm shall befall you."

The Prior of Emmett was not happy when Sir Richard paid his debt. The prior had counted on seizing the knight's castle because it was worth much more than the four hundred pounds Sir Richard owed.

True to his word, Sir Richard of the Lea returned to Sherwood Forest one year and one day later. He counted out five hundred golden pounds to Robin Hood. He also brought gifts for Robin and all his men: fine Spanish bows inlaid with silver. With them came quivers of arrows embroidered in gold.

That was not the last the men would see of Sir Richard of the Lea. Soon enough, he repaid his debt to Robin Hood yet again.

CHAPTER 14

Guy of Gisbourne Meets His Fate

Oftentimes, the sun shines brightly on the morning before a big storm. Such was the case on Robin Hood's darkest day since turning outlaw. The birds twittered in the trees, and gentle breezes ruffled the leaves. Little John and Robin Hood talked as they strolled through the forest.

"We've had no adventures in some time," Little John complained. "I think we should each set out alone and see what we can find. When we come back together, we shall have merry tales to tell."

"I like your plan, Little John," said Robin.

They reached a fork in the path, and Robin pointed to the left. "You go that way, and I will go this way. I'm sure you won't find any trouble you can't handle."

As Robin walked eagerly along his path, thinking of adventure, he suddenly spied an evil-looking man sitting beneath a big oak tree. From head to toe, the man wore a heavy cloak of dark horsehide. A hood made from the skin of the horse's head hid his face from view. The ears on the hood stood up like horns. By the man's side lay a sword and a longbow. He wore a quiver of arrows across his back.

Robin was a bit frightened, but he called out cheerfully, "Hello, who sits there? And what do you wear on your body? If I had done something wrong, I'd worry that you had been sent by the devil to take my soul."

The stranger slowly turned and looked at

Robin; then he pushed the hood back on his head. His eyes were hard and dark. "Who are you?" he growled.

"Speak not so sourly, brother," answered Robin. "Did you eat thorns and vinegar for breakfast today?"

The stranger growled back, "If you do not like my words, leave now. I assure you that my deeds match my speech."

"Oh, but I do like your words, you sweet, pretty thing," Robin said, smiling. "Your speech is as witty and bright as any I've heard in my life."

The stranger stared at Robin with a wicked look. Robin returned the stare, grinning all the while. Finally, the stranger broke the silence. "What is your name?"

"I am glad to hear you speak!" exclaimed Robin. "I was beginning to think you had been struck dumb. Now, as for my name, it might be this and it might be that. But I think it's more fitting for you to tell me *your* name because you are the stranger in these parts."

The stranger laughed with a cold, rough sound. "I do not know why I don't cut you down. Two days ago I skewered a man in Nottingham town for less. I am Guy of Gisbourne, an outlaw. The Sheriff of Nottingham will give me free pardon for my past crimes plus two hundred pounds to kill a certain outlaw by the name of Robin Hood. 'Set a thief to catch a thief,' the saying goes."

As Robin listened, he felt his heart rise in his chest. Guy of Gisbourne's murderous deeds were infamous throughout England. But Robin continued to smile. "Truly, I have heard of your gentle doings. I believe there is no one in the world whom Robin Hood would rather meet."

Gisbourne let out another harsh laugh. "It is merry to think of two stout outlaws meeting each other, but it will be a very ill day for Robin Hood. The day he meets me will be the day he dies."

"But, gentle soul," Robin said, "don't you think that Robin Hood may be the better man? I know him right well. Many hereabouts think he is the stoutest man alive."

"He may be the stoutest man hereabouts," said Gisbourne scornfully, "but hereabouts is not the wide world. They call him an outlaw, yet Robin Hood has not shed blood since fleeing to the forest. They call him an archer, but I would not be afraid to stand against him with a bow in my hand any day."

"Truly they call him a great archer. We of Nottinghamshire are famous with the longbow. Even I, a simple hand at the craft, would not fear to try a bout with you."

Gisbourne laughed coarsely. "I like your spirit. Put up a wreath."

"Oh, no," protested Robin. "Only little children shoot at garlands in these woods. Stay here, and I will set a good Nottingham target."

Robin stepped off the path and cut a stick from a hazel thicket. He sharpened one end and stuck it in the ground in front of an oak tree. Then he measured off eighty paces. "There. That is the kind of mark Nottingham men shoot at. Let me see you split the wand if you call yourself an archer."

"The devil himself could not hit that mark," complained Gisbourne.

"Perhaps he could and perhaps he could not," Robin replied. "We will never know until you shoot."

Gisbourne picked up his bow. His first arrow missed the hazel wand by a foot. He shot again, missing the wand by six inches.

Robin laughed merrily. "I see now that the devil himself *cannot* hit that mark. Let's see if I can."

Robin drew his bow and shot quickly. His arrow sliced straight through the air and split the wand where it stood.

Before Guy of Gisbourne could speak, Robin flung his bow to the ground. Drawing his sword, he shouted fiercely, "There, bloody villain! Now you've seen how little you know of manly sports. Look last on the daylight, vile beast. Today you die! I am Robin Hood!"

Gisbourne was stunned. "Are you indeed Robin Hood? I am very glad to meet you. Say your prayers!" Gisbourne unsheathed his sword.

Then began the fiercest fight that Sherwood had ever seen. Drops of red blood soon sprinkled the ground, but none came from Robin's veins. At last, Gisbourne lunged. Robin dodged the thrust by lightly stepping backward, but his heel caught on a root and he tumbled onto his back. "God help me now," prayed Robin.

Gisbourne stabbed furiously at Robin. He caught the blade with his bare hand. Though it cut him deeply, Robin was able to push the sword away and drive it into the ground. Then he leapt

up and raised his sword. Gisbourne tried to pull his sword from the earth, but Robin's blade slashed under Gisbourne's arm. Gisbourne spun around, and Robin plunged hot steel through his enemy's innards. Gisbourne screamed as he collapsed and fell to the green grass.

Robin wiped his sword clean. As he stood over Gisbourne's body, Robin thought, "This is the first man I have slain since my youth. I often think bitterly of that day. But this killing was justified. The Sheriff of Nottingham sent this evil man against me. I will wear Gisbourne's garments and find the sheriff. Perhaps I can repay him the deed somehow."

CHAPTER 15

Robin "Repays" the Sheriff

༄

While Robin was fighting Guy of Gisbourne, Little John had found his own trouble on the left fork of the path. Walking past a house, he heard someone sobbing. An old woman answered his knock. Tears streamed from her eyes. "Dear woman," Little John said, "what troubles you? Perhaps I can help."

The woman looked up at Little John. "I don't think even Robin Hood himself could help me, but I will tell you my story. I am a widow with three sons. Last night, my oldest killed a deer. The sheriff's men followed the drops of blood on the forest floor to my cottage. The Sheriff of Nottingham vows to hang my boys from a tree at the edge of Sherwood Forest."

Little John listened carefully. "Ah," he said, "I know the sheriff well. I also know how to set your sons free." He told the women that he needed a disguise. She gave him her dead husband's clothes to wear. Then Little John made himself a false beard and wig from white sheep's wool. Pretending to be an old man, he walked to the edge of the forest.

The sheriff, seated on his horse, saw John coming and called out, "Old man, come here! How would you like to earn sixpence?"

"Sixpence! Why, yes, sir! What is it needs doing?"

The sheriff pointed at the three boys. Their hands were tied behind their backs. "These rascals need hanging. I'll pay you six pennies for the work."

"Gladly, sir," agreed Little John. "Sixpence is a fair sum for such easy work. Have these naughty fellows confessed their sins?"

"You can try your hand as a confessor if you'd like," said the sheriff impatiently, "so long as you're quick about it."

"May I string my bow, good master?" asked Little John. "I'd like to tickle their ribs with an arrow while they dangle."

"Do whatever you like," barked the sheriff. "Just get the job done quickly."

Little John strung his bow. Then he went over to each boy and pretended to hear his confession. "I will cut your bonds," he whispered. "Keep your hands together so no one notices. When I say *run*, dash into the forest." John freed the third boy's bonds, then fitted an arrow into his bow. He drew the bow halfway back and shouted, "Run!"

All three boys sprinted into the woods. Little

John slowly backed up toward the safety of the forest, keeping his arrow trained on the sheriff's men. "Whoever takes one step toward me dies," he warned. No one moved.

The sheriff suddenly recognized Little John and flew into a rage. Spurring his horse, the sheriff drew his sword and descended on John like the wind.

Little John pulled back on his bowstring, ready to shoot. Crack! His bow split in his hand. He threw the shattered bow at the sheriff's horse, but the sheriff kept coming. Swinging his sword as hard as he could, the sheriff hit Little John on the head with the flat side of the blade. The blow knocked Little John to the ground, where he lay unconscious.

Jumping off his horse, the sheriff exulted, "Oh, this is a happy day! I happily trade those poachers for Robin Hood's right-hand man! Let us hang this rogue today before his master has a chance to aid him. We will leave his body as a warning to all others of his ilk."

As the sheriff's men prepared the hanging tree, a dark figure appeared on the road. "Isn't that Guy of Gisbourne there?" asked one of the men fearfully

The sheriff looked up. He saw the dark horse-hide cloak smeared with blood. A chill ran down his spine, for even the sheriff feared Guy of Gisbourne. "Yes, that is the devil. I hope he slew the master thief."

Little John groaned and began to wake up. When he saw the figure walking down the road, his heart sank. The man carried Robin's bugle and bow, and his clothes were covered in blood.

"How now!" cried the sheriff. "What luck did you have in the forest? Why, man, your clothes are covered in blood!"

Robin answered in a harsh voice like

Gisbourne's so that the sheriff would not know him. "If you do not like my clothes, you can shut your eyes. The blood on me is that of the vilest outlaw that ever lived. I have slain him today."

Little John cried out, "Oh, you vile wretch! I know you, Guy of Gisbourne. Truly you are a fit tool for a coward like the Sheriff of Nottingham. I will die gladly, life means nothing to me now." Hot tears rolled down Little John's cheeks as he spoke.

The sheriff said, glee in his voice, "Tell me this is true, Guy of Gisbourne."

"What I tell you is true. Here is Robin Hood's sword, his bow, and his bugle. Do you think he would give them to me freely?"

The sheriff clapped his hands. "The great outlaw is dead, and his right-hand man is mine! Ask for whatever you like, Guy of Gisbourne. I will give it to you."

"Give me this man's life," Robin demanded.

"As I have slain the master, I would slay the man."

"You are a fool," laughed the sheriff. "I would have given you whatever money you desired. But I have promised, so you may have him."

"I thank you for the gift," Robin said. "Now lean the man against that tree. I'll show you how we handle things where I come from."

While the sheriff's men busied themselves with Little John, Robin strung the two bows he carried. Then he walked toward Little John.

The sheriff's men backed up. Little John shouted, "Come! Here is my chest. It is right that the same hand that murdered my master should butcher me! I know you, Guy of Gisbourne!"

"Peace, Little John," Robin whispered. "You've said twice that you know me, but you do not know me at all. Just over there is a bow and my broadsword. When I cut your bonds, grab them quickly. Now! Get them!"

In the same instant, Robin swiftly fitted an

arrow to the string of his bow. "The first man who touches a sword or a bowstring dies! I have killed Guy of Gisbourne. Be careful that it is not your turn next!"

The sheriff cried out, "Robin Hood!" He was sure that Robin would kill him that day. The sheriff turned his horse and kicked it with his spurs. It sprinted off in a cloud of dust.

The horse was fast but not faster than an arrow. With a twang of his bow, Little John sent a shaft zipping through the air. Thwack! The arrow lodged in the sheriff's behind, sticking out like the tail feathers of a sparrow. For the next month, the sheriff was very sore indeed and could sit only on the softest cushions.

CHAPTER 16

King Richard Dines in
Sherwood Forest

After the death of good King Henry, his son Richard, known as Lionheart because of his bravery on the battlefield, took the throne. He decided to make a royal tour across England so that he could better get to know both the country and his subjects. Everyone felt sure that he would visit Nottingham on his journey.

Soon messengers went riding back and forth between the sheriff and the king, until at last a date was agreed on for the king to come to Nottingham.

To prepare for the king's arrival, great arches were built across the streets that Richard would pass, and many of these arches were draped with silk banners and streamers of many colors. In the town's Guild Hall, where a great feast was being prepared, the best carpenters built a throne where the king would sit at the head of the table, with the sheriff at his side.

On the morning of King Richard's visit, the bright sun shone down into the stony streets, now alive with a restless sea of people, country and town folk alike. They were packed together so close that the sheriff's men could hardly push them back to leave space for the king's path. Among the crowd stood many men in Lincoln green, for Robin and his companions greatly admired their new king.

After a long wait, the clear sounds of many bugles came winding down the street, and all the people turned their heads and began looking in the direction from which the sounds came.

At long last, the king's men-at-arms galloped into the center of town as all the people began to cheer. Never had Nottingham seen a more wonderful sight than when a hundred noble knights, all dressed in polished armor that sparkled brightly in the sun, proudly rode down the streets. The clattering sounds that the massive hooves of their great warhorses made on the cobblestone only added to the marvel.

Behind the valiant knights came the great nobles of the land, dressed in robes made of silk and gold, and with golden chains around their neck. They were followed by vast swarm of men-at-arms holding spears in their hands as they marched past the crowd.

In the midst of this procession came two riders, side by side. One of them was the Sheriff of Nottingham, dressed in the great robes of his office. The other, who was a head taller than the sheriff, wore a rich but simple garb, with a broad, heavy chain around his neck. His hair and beard were like gold and his eyes were as blue as the summer sky. As he rode along, he bowed first to the right and then to the left. A mighty roar of voices followed him as he passed; for this was King Richard. Robin and his men cheered the king the loudest.

That night the great dinner to honor King Richard's visit was held in the Guild Hall. A thousand lights gleamed along a huge table, where lords and nobles and knights feasted with delight. At the head of the table, upon a throne covered with gold cloth, sat King Richard, with the Sheriff of Nottingham just beside him.

After a time, King Richard turned to the sheriff and said, "I have heard about a band of outlaws in these parts, led by a man named Robin Hood. Can you tell me anything about him?"

Hearing these words, the sheriff's face turned

gloomy. He then said, "I can tell your majesty little about those naughty rogues, except that they are the boldest lawbreakers in the land."

One of the king's favorite men, Sir Henry of the Lea, now spoke up. "May it please your majesty," he said, "when I was away in France, I often heard from my father. Most of the time my father told me about this very fellow, Robin Hood. If your majesty would like, I will tell you a certain adventure of this outlaw."

Then the king, with a smile on his face, gave permission to Sir Henry to continue. Sir Henry then spoke about how Robin Hood had helped his father, Sir Richard of the Lea. King Richard laughed when he heard that Robin Hood had used the Bishop of Hereford's money to pay Sir Richard's debts. The bishop, who sat beside the king, turned redder and redder with each sentence.

Seeing how much the king had truly enjoyed

such a merry tale, others at the table also began to tell stories about Robin Hood. "By the hilt of my sword," the king declared after hearing their stories, "this is the boldest merry knave I have ever heard of."

Later that night, the king sat up talking with Sir Henry and some of his other knights. His mind was still on Robin Hood. "I would give one hundred pounds to meet this Robin Hood and see some of his doings in Sherwood Forest."

Sir Hubert laughed. "If your majesty would truly like to meet Robin Hood, I can arrange it. If your majesty is willing to lose one hundred pounds, you can not only meet this fellow, but you can also feast with him in Sherwood Forest."

"How can we do that?" asked the king.

"Your majesty, we will dress as friars. You will wear a purse containing one hundred pounds. Then we will take the road through Sherwood Forest to Mansfield town tomorrow. Before the day is ended, we will meet Robin Hood and dine with him."

"I like your plan!" the king said happily. "We set forth tomorrow."

The next morning, just as King Richard and his men were preparing to leave, the Sheriff of Nottingham came to visit. After the king told him about the plan to meet Robin Hood, the sheriff drew the king aside for a private talk. "Your majesty, you are riding into danger," the sheriff warned. "O my great lord and king, this villain Robin Hood has no respect either for the king or the king's law."

"But Robin Hood has shed no blood since he was outlawed, except, or so I have heard, for that of Guy of Gisbourne," replied the king. "And Guy was such an evil rogue that all honest men should thank Robin."

"Yes, your majesty," the sheriff answered. "You have heard correctly. Nevertheless—"

"What then do I have to fear?" asked the king, interrupting the sheriff. "I have done him no harm. Truly, there is no danger in this. But perhaps you will come with us, sir sheriff."

The sheriff turned white just at the very thought of an encounter with Robin. "Heaven forbid!" he cried.

King Richard and his men then rode out of Nottingham. They put the hoods of their robes over their faces so that no one would recognize them. After they had been on the road for some time, the king grew thirsty. "I would give fifty pounds for something to soothe my parched throat," he cried.

Instantly, a blond man with dazzling blue eyes jumped into the road and grabbed the bridle of the king's horse. "Truly, holy brother, it would be wrong to deny your wish. We keep an inn here. For fifty pounds, we will give you a good drink and a noble feast." Robin put his bugle to his lips and blew. The bushes rustled, and sixty men in Lincoln green popped up on both sides of the road.

"Who are you, naughty rogue?" King Richard demanded. "Don't you have any respect for holy men?"

"Not a bit," answered Robin. "As for my name, it is Robin Hood. You may have heard of me."

"Out upon thee," said King Richard. "You are a bold and naughty fellow, and a lawless one, too. Now let me and my brothers pass in peace."

"We can't let such holy men travel with empty stomachs," protested Robin. "Show me your purse, reverend brother, or I may have to strip your robes from you to search for it myself."

"No, use no force," the king said sternly. "Here is my purse. Don't lay your lawless hands on my person."

"Tut tut," chided Robin Hood. "Whom do

you think you are? Are you the king of England to talk like that to me?" Robin Hood handed the purse to Will Scarlet for counting.

When Will had finished, Robin stuffed fifty pounds into his pockets and gave the other fifty back to the king. "Here, brother, take back half your money. Will you put back your hood? I would like to see your face."

"No," said the king. "I may not put back my hood. We seven have taken a vow that we will not show our faces for twenty-four hours."

"Then keep them covered in peace," Robin said. "I would never ask you to break your vow."

When they reached the Greenwood Tree, Robin told his men to bring glasses of drink. Then he raised a toast. "Here is to good King Richard. May all his enemies be dashed to the ground."

All drank to the king's health, even King Richard. "I think, good fellow," he said, "that you have drunk to your own dashing."

"No," said Robin. "We of Sherwood are loyal to our lord. We would give our very lives for him."

The king laughed. "Perhaps King Richard's health and happiness is more to me than you know. But enough of that matter. We have paid well for our fare, so can you not show us some sport?"

"We are always happy to please our guests," Robin said agreeably. "Lads! Set up a garland at the end of the glade."

Swiftly, the men hung a wreath of leaves and flowers from a stake on a broad tree trunk. Robin Hood called out the rules. "There is a fair mark, lads. Each shoots three arrows. If any fellow misses, he will get a swat from Will Scarlet's fist."

"Listen to him," cried Friar Tuck. "Why, master, you give away swats from your strapping nephew as if they were love taps from a young girl!"

David of Duncaster shot first. All three arrows

struck within the ring of the wreath. Then Midge the miller shot. He also hit the mark every time. Wat the tinker followed, but his luck was bad. One of his arrows missed the wreath by an inch.

"Come here, fellow," Will Scarlet said in a soft, gentle voice. "I owe you something that I would like to pay you." Wat braced for the blow, closing his eyes tightly. Will Scarlet reared back, then swung his arm. "Whoof!" his palm smacked Wat in the head, and the tinker tumbled to the grass.

As Wat sat rubbing his ear, everyone roared. King Richard laughed until tears ran down his cheeks. The men continued their sport, and most of the merry men hit the target. Some missed and suffered the same fate Wat had.

Robin's turn came last. His first arrow split a piece from the stake that held the wreath. The second arrow struck within an inch of the first. The king thought, "I would give one thousand pounds to have this fellow as one of my guard!"

Robin's third arrow was poorly feathered, though. It wobbled in midair and struck the tree an inch outside the wreath.

The men sitting on the ground rolled around with laughter. They had never before seen their master miss his target by so much. Robin flung his bow down and declared, "That arrow had a bad feather! Give me another, and I will split a stick with it."

Everyone laughed louder than ever. "No, good uncle," said Will Scarlet sweetly. "You had a fair chance. Come here. I owe you something, and I would like to pay."

"Go, good master," roared Friar Tuck. "You have bestowed these love taps of Will Scarlet's with great freedom. It would be a pity if you did not get your share."

"It may not be," Robin protested. "I am king here, and no subject may raise a hand against a king. But even our great King Richard may yield to a churchman without shame. I will yield myself to this holy friar." Robin turned to the king. "I ask you, brother, will you take my punishment into your holy hands?"

"With all my heart," said King Richard. "I owe you something for taking a weight of fifty pounds from my purse."

"If you make me tumble, I will give back your fifty pounds. But if I don't feel grass against my back," Robin warned, "I will take every penny you have."

"I am willing to venture it," agreed the king. He rolled up his sleeve and cocked his arm. Robin stood before him, his feet planted wide, smiling. Then King Richard delivered a blow like a thunderbolt and knocked Robin to the grass. His men clutched their stomachs in laughter.

Robin sat up, looking as though he had been dropped from a cloud. Finally, he said, "Will Scarlet, count this fellow out fifty pounds. I want nothing more of either him or his money. I should have taken my punishment from you. I believe I'm deaf in one ear now."

The king bowed to Robin. "I thank you, fellow. If you should ever wish for another box on the ear, I will give it to you for nothing."

Suddenly, all heard a horse pounding through the forest. Sir Richard of the Lea galloped into the glade. "Make haste, dear friend!" he shouted breathlessly. "King Richard left Nottingham town this very morning, looking for you. Gather your band and come with me to the Castle on the Lea." Sir Richard pulled up short and stared at the men dressed as friars. "Who are these strangers?"

"Why," answered Robin, rising from the grass, "these are some gentle guests we found on the high road. I don't know their names, but I've become well acquainted with this rogue's palm."

Sir Richard looked keenly at the tall friar. The

friar stood up to his full height and held Sir Richard's eyes. Suddenly, Sir Richard's cheeks grew pale. He leapt off his horse and dropped to his knees. The friar threw back his hood.

"How dare you offer your castle, Sir Richard?" King Richard demanded sternly. "Will you make it a hiding place for the most well-known outlaws in England?"

Sir Richard raised his eyes to the king. "I would never do anything to anger your majesty, but I would sooner suffer your wrath than see any harm come to Robin Hood and his band. I owe them life, honor, everything. Should I desert them in their hour of need?"

As the knight finished speaking, one of the mock friars came forward and knelt beside Sir Richard. He threw back his hood, and Sir Richard recognized the face of his son. Sir Henry of the Lea said, "Here I kneel, King Richard. I have served you well. I have stepped between you and death,

but I must tell you that I, too, would shelter
Robin Hood. My father's honor is as dear to me as
my own."

King Richard looked slowly around. Then his
frown curled into a smile. "Your son takes after
you in action and speech," he said to Sir Richard.
"It is true what he says. He did save my life in battle. For that reason, I would pardon you, Sir
Richard, even if you had done worse. Rise, all of
you! You will suffer no harm from me today. It
would be a pity to spoil such a merry time."

The king called Robin over. "How are you? Is
your ear still too deaf to hear me speak?"

"My ears would be deafened in death before
they would cease to hear your majesty's voice,"
said Robin.

"But for my mercy and the loyalty to me you
spoke of earlier, I might have closed your ears for
good," said King Richard, with some coldness in
his voice. "The danger is passed. I give you and all

your band free pardon. I would like to take you into my guard, along with Little John, your cousin Will Scarlet, and your minstrel, Allan a Dale. As for the rest, we will appoint them royal rangers. They will be law-abiding caretakers of our deer in Sherwood rather than outlawed poachers. Now, ready a feast, for I would like to see how you live in these woodlands."

That night, King Richard slept on a bed of tender green leaves. The next morning, the famous outlaws marched into town with the king. A day later, Robin Hood, Little John, and Will Scarlet said good-bye to their old friends. They hugged them and shook their hands, promising to return often to Sherwood. Then each man mounted a horse and proudly rode off to serve his king.

Questions, Questions, Questions

by Arthur Pober, Ed.D.

Have you ever been around a toddler who keeps asking the question "Why?" Does your teacher call on you in class with questions from your homework? Do your parents ask you questions at the dinner table about your day? We are always surrounded by questions that need a specific response. But is it possible to have a question with no right answer?

The following questions are about the book you just read. But this is not a quiz! They are designed to help you look at the people, places, and events in the story from different angles. These questions do not have specific answers. Instead, they might make you think of the story in a completely new way.

Think carefully about each question and enjoy discovering more about this classic story.

1. Many of Robin's men have special names or nicknames. If you had to choose names for your family or friends, what might they be? Do you have a nickname?

2. The prize for the winner of the sheriff's shooting contest was a golden arrow. Do you think it was the prize that appealed to Robin about the contest or was it something else?

3. The sheriff said that Robin's men feared nothing. Do you think this is true? Can you think of any instances when they were afraid? Do you know anyone who fears nothing?

4. Robin tells the sheriff that he "should never

buy a horse without first looking it in the mouth." What does he mean? Do you agree with him?

5. Does Will's story of being charged with murder sound very much like "history repeating itself"? What do you think this phrase means?

6. Robin tricks Friar Tuck into carrying him across the river on his shoulders. How do you feel about Robin and Friar Tuck's behavior? Do they deserve what they got from each other?

7. Robin tells the bishop that "the bride will love her man as long as they both live." How could he have been so sure? Did you know what Robin planned to do?

8. Sir Richard gives Robin his knightly word. What do you think this means? Is there an equivalent of that today?

9. In many of his adventures, Robin seems to get outsmarted. Why do you think that happens?

Did you realize what was happening before Robin did?

10. Robin can sometimes be self-centered. Do you agree? In what parts of the story do you see this behavior? Do you know anyone like Robin?

Afterword

⁓

First impressions are important.

Whether we are meeting new people, going to new places, or picking up a book unknown to us, first impressions count for a lot. They can lead to warm, lasting memories or can make us shy away from any future encounters.

Can you recall your own first impressions and earliest memories of reading the classics?

Do you remember wading through pages and pages of text to prepare for an exam? Or were you the child who hid under the blanket to read with a flashlight, joining forces with Robin Hood to save Maid Marian? Do you remember only how long it took you to read a lengthy novel such as *Little Women*? Or did you become best friends with the March sisters?

Even for a gifted young reader, getting through long chapters with dense language can easily become overwhelming and can obscure the richness of the story and its characters. Reading an abridged, newly crafted version of a classic novel can be the gentle introduction a child needs to explore the characters and story line without the frustration of difficult vocabulary and complex themes.

Reading an abridged version of a classic novel gives the young reader a sense of independence and the satisfaction of finishing a "grown-up" book. And when a child is engaged with and inspired by a classic story, the tone is set for further exploration of the story's themes, characters, history, and details. As a child's reading skills advance, the desire to tackle the original, unabridged version of the story will naturally emerge.

If made accessible to young readers, these stories can become invaluable tools for understanding themselves in the context of their families and social environments. This is why the Classic Starts series includes questions that stimulate discussion regarding the impact and social relevance of the characters and stories today. These questions can foster lively conversations between children and their parents or teachers. When we look at the issues, values, and standards of past times in terms of how we live now, we can appreciate literature's classic tales in a very personal and engaging way.

Share your love of reading the classics with a young child, and introduce an imaginary world real enough to last a lifetime.

DR. ARTHUR POBER, ED.D.

Dr. Arthur Pober has spent more than twenty years in the fields of early-childhood and gifted education. He is the former principal of one of the world's oldest laboratory schools for gifted youngsters, Hunter College Elementary School, and former director of Magnet Schools for the Gifted and Talented for more than 25,000 youngsters in New York City.

Dr. Pober is a recognized authority in the areas of media and child protection and is currently the U.S. representative to the European Institute for the Media and European Advertising Standards Alliance.